What are godmothers for?

Written by Hannah Harrison
Illustrated by Savannah Betten

ISBN 978-1-68197-020-2 (paperback)
ISBN 978-1-68197-021-9 (digital)

Copyright © 2015 by Hannah Harrison

All rights reserved. No part of this publication may be reproduced, distributed, or transmitted in any form or by any means, including photocopying, recording, or other electronic or mechanical methods without the prior written permission of the publisher. For permission requests, solicit the publisher via the address below.

Christian Faith Publishing, Inc.
296 Chestnut Street
Meadville, PA 16335
www.christianfaithpublishing.com
Printed in the United States of America

For Carol Ann and Jase

What are godmothers for?

Godmothers are for going on adventures.

Godmothers are for celebrating special occasions...

... And for always calling on your birthday.

Godmothers are for giving BIG surprises!

Godmothers are for making you try new things...

... and helping you with hard decisions.

Godmothers are for taking lots of pictures...

Godmothers are for picking you up when you feel down....

... and sometimes even letting you wear a crown!

Godmothers are for inspiring your imagination....

... and for making silly faces!

Godmothers are for helping you make friends with animals...

.... And for taking you on awesome day trips!

Godmothers are for teaching you new things...

.... And for throwing the most fun parties!

But most of all.....

Godmothers are for LOVING you, no matter what!

The End

www.ingramcontent.com/pod-product-compliance
Ingram Content Group UK Ltd.
Pitfield, Milton Keynes, MK11 3LW, UK
UKHW061623240426
12048UKWH00050B/1679